ALLELUIA

POETRY, LYRICS AND PROSE INTENDED
TO DRAW YOU CLOSER TO JESUS

KATHLEEN JAMES

ISBN
978-1-959314-26-4 (Paperback)
978-1-959314-27-1 (eBook)

Alleluia

Poetry, Lyrics and Prose Intended to Draw You Closer to Jesus.

By Kathleen James

Cover photo: The Flammarion Woodcut

I would like to dedicate this book to my Lord and Savior
Jesus Christ and to all of my loved ones. To all the little ones,
especially those in need. And of course, to the lost.

Please join with me in prayer

Dear Heavenly Father,

With tender mercy and loving kindness, draw us into your

Kingdom. Draw us to Christ.

Break every stronghold separating us from you. Protect us

from all evil.

In Jesus name we pray,
Thank you and Amen

Table of Contents

Pentecost

A tongue of fire will descend

Engulfed in joy that never ends

Your heart will grow

Your words have wings

You'll have a knowing in all things

Heart of rock turns to flesh

Forever to walk in joy and happiness

Never alone

Never again

When the Holy Spirit descends

Alleluia

The King

The King is coming
Prepare the way
This is the dawn
Of a great and glorious day

Receive his message
Receive his grace
For very soon
You will see his face

The time has come
The drum roll has begun
Tell your friends
Tell everyone

You don't need silver
You don't need gold
Your heart is the prize
He wants to hold

In all his glory
In all his might
All the world rejoice
The coming of the light

———

Kathleen James

Look

Look at him
The Holy One
The Father, Spirit, and the Son

There is a mystery you cannot see
Look at him This is the key

Look at him
The Three in One
You are better off each time you do

Trust me
I'm telling you
The Truth

Look at him
Take the time
There is a mystery
You cannot see

Look at him
This is the key

Alleluia

Do You Want to Know?

If I had the answer
Should I let you know?

If I knew the way
Should I take you there?

If I had the key
Should I unlock the door?

Kathleen James

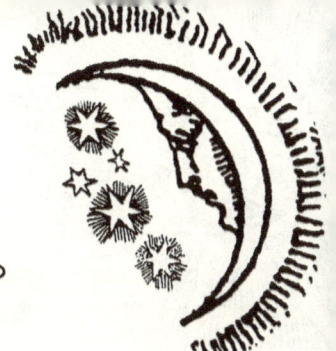

Do Not Fear

He is coming for you, my darling

He is coming for you, my dear

He is coming to hold you close

To always have you near

If you cannot find him

Do not be dismayed

His angel will take you by the hand

And lead you to his grace

Glories are before you

Joys you have never known

As you are with the master

Sitting on his throne

When he hesitated, the men grasped his hand and the hands of his
wife and of his two daughters and led them safely out of the city,
for the Lord was merciful to them. (Gen. 19:16)

And he will send his angles with a loud trumpet call, and they will
gather his elect from the four winds, from one end of the heavens
to the other. (Mat. 24:31)

Alleluia

A Favorite Prayer

Heavenly Father, before I take another breath
I'm asking you this day to bless.

A Favorite Prayer

Bless Bless Bless

Kathleen James

You Can Do It

What's in your heart?
What's in your hands?

Start where you are
Use what you have
Do what you can

What's in your heart?
What's in your hands?

Heaven

I have come to realize something important.

Are you going to be there?

Are the ones you love

Going to be there?

Everything else pales in comparison.

Kathleen James

The Keys

There is a song waiting to be sung

About the keys to thy kingdom come

A place where sweet perfume fills the air

A place of tender warmth and loving care

Oh, but how to enter in

And rid ourselves of awful sin

He has the keys in his hand

He is in charge

He is in command

To His Majesty you must go

And there a better friend you will find

Than any you have left behind

All, yes all, who come to him

He will let enter in

Alleluia

Speak

Continue to speak, dear one

Continue to act on my behalf

Your heartfelt testimony is needed now

Remember the when

Remember the how

Kathleen James

My Testimony

I was 28, trying to make an important decision. I tossed all the options around, trying to look at it from every angle. I had made some poor decisions in the past and this time I wanted to make the best decision. Then I thought,

What would Jesus do if he were standing in my shoes?

I decided I would figure out how Jesus would handle it and that's how I would handle it. Then it happened. Some people call it *an outpouring of the spirit*, some call it *born again*.

My faith and entry into heaven had already been secured. I had been baptized long ago. I had asked for forgiveness of my sins and accepted Christ as my savior long ago. I had called on Jesus many times before. God had visited me and communicated with me many times before.

But this was the most amazing moment of my life. The presence of God engulfed me. I guess that's what was meant by *a tongue of fire.* I was permeated with joy and euphoria. I knew God was with me and loved me.

I remember thinking *all the people wanting to make contact with life in outer space and I just made contact.* Do you remember the movie *The Blues Brothers* when they were in church and saw the light? Do you remember in the movie *The Grinch* when the Grinch's heart grew

Alleluia

three sizes? My hand was fractured and in a cast. I was so confident, I took my cast off.

And the decision I was trying to make? It was trivial and of no importance in the presence of God. I never made a decision about the issue, I just walked over it.

Kathleen James

Start Walking

Thank God I am so blessed. God said I would
live abundantly and I have. For example, the
medical report was bad. Never knew it till I saw the
report. The report said I had a stroke. The report
said I had fractured my neck and back. I lived
anyway--went swimming this week.

The financial report was bad. Started out as a
teenage mother, need I say more? My Scott and I,
we raised four awesome kids--the joy of my life,
anyway. I met a lady once who had ten kids. She
told me God will provide. She said every time she
had a baby, she was amazed, there was always room
for one more.

Just start walking with God, then
fifty-eight years will go by and you will marvel.
You live anyway.

Alleluia

13

Cindy

Been walking the walk
And talking the talk
Then my friend
Put me on the spot

Pray for me she said
I have a need she begged
You see the Holy Spirit
Sent me to you

So, we prayed together
Me and her
And the cloud descended
True to his word

So she left
Happy and healed
I was left with
Great joy and zeal

Kathleen James

Then it happened
The very next day
Satan came to take

My joy away

I was sick
I was ill
This must be stopped
No light on a hill

But he was too late
He is going to lose
I have already fought him
A time or two

For when I did
All I could
And trusted and stood
God came through

So who gets the glory
Not Satan
Not me
Jesus Christ is the one to whom
Glory, Glory Be

Alleluia

15

What I Want

I want to talk to God
I want to hear
What he has to say

I want to know
What he is doing
What is on his mind today

I want to walk with God
And do the things he does

I want to go where he goes
And show his acts of love

I want to see him face to face
I saw him once in a dream

Come near me, God
Come to me
Visit me today

Kathleen James

Fear Not

My love, my crystal dove

Fear not my plans for thee

Your morning cry

Was heard on high

On wings

Your victory

Alleluia

17

Treasure

My fire is lit
Can you see
The fire burning
Inside of me

My fire is lit
This is true
This fire is also
For you too

You knew me then
You know me now

Tell me
What could make
This change
Come about

Seek the answer
You will find
Treasure
Treasure Divine

Kathleen James

Then you too will want to tell
The world about his glories and yell
I have good news! I have good news!
I have good news! Good news for you!

Alleluia

Alleluia

Allelu

Alleluia

Luia

Alleluia

He walks through the future
He walks through the past

He knows what you need
Before you ask

Like water taking any shape
Living water is his name

He is made out of love
He is made out of grace

So powerful you can't
Look at his face

Have no fear
No worry
No strife

Kathleen James

He wants to give you abundant life

Allelu

Alleluia

Luia

Alleluia

Alleluia

Important

When My eyes were opened and I understood God, Christ and the Spirit, I was content. I went for many, many years happy and satisfied. I kept it to myself because the world did not understand. So I lived in peace in a world full of chaos. Usually if something was not right, I went around it, taking solace in the fact that I could always turn to God.

But this has changed. Here it is thirty years later and I have had a change of heart. Maybe it is because of all the end of the world talk. Maybe it is because I have realized just how important it really is. Now I realize I can no longer stay silent.

It is for your sake I speak up. It would be so much easier to keep it to myself. But if I loved you, if I really really loved you, I would see to it you know the truth so that your eyes may also be opened. Think about it. Are you going to be there? (In heaven)? Are your loved ones going to be there? Everything else pales in comparison. This is the only thing that matters in this life.

It is promised; Call on Jesus and you will be saved.

The kingdom of God is so rich and powerful, limitless. Ever expanding forever and ever in every direction in every dimension. We really cannot comprehend it. I delight in this and my growth in it...but--

---

Kathleen James

22

What really matters is getting into the kingdom. Here is what you have to do. It is written and promised to us: Call on Jesus and you will be saved.

Hold on to that promise. Hide it in your heart. Don't let anyone talk you out of it. Don't let anyone steal this from you. It's the most important thing you will ever do.

Here is an example of how to do it: Why don't you do it right now? Close your eyes, bow your head, say, "Jesus I'm calling on you." That's it. That's all you have to do. Now, hold on to that promise for dear life.

I must warn you. There is so much more. You may find yourself wanting to know more about the Kingdom, to open your eyes. And that liar Satan will try to destroy you. But hold on to that promise no matter what and I promise. You will be all right.

It would also help to pray--for help, and to help others--is a good place to start. And read the Bible. I cannot stress that enough. Read the Bible. Put on the full armor of God.

Once your eyes are opened and you realize, you will be so thankful and grateful you will not want to break God's laws out of gratitude and not because you are forced to. And you will do this so imperfectly. But God is perfect for us. In the end he will perfect us.

And everyone who calls on the name of the Lord will be saved; for on Mount Zion and in Jerusalem there will be deliverance, as

Alleluia

the Lord has said, even among the survivors whom the Lord calls (Joel 2:32)

For "Everyone who calls on the name of the Lord will be saved. (Rom. 10:13)

And everyone who calls on the name of the Lord will be saved (Acts 2:21)

You know with all your heart and soul that not one of all the good promises the Lord your God gave you has failed. Every promise has been fullfilled: not one has failed. (Josh. 23:14)

Only One Way

There is only one way
To Our Father
It's through Jesus Christ
Our Lord

What gives me the right
To offend you in this way
To be so bold and tell you
There is only one way

Your eternal destiny is at stake
So, I must speak up and say
Separation from the Father
Surely would be hell

Go to the Bible
To John 14:6
And read it for yourself

We belong together
You, the Father, and I
He created us
He gave us life

Jesus answered, "I am the way and the truth and the life. No one comes to the Father except through me." (John 14:6)

———————

Alleluia

25

Christmas Bells

Christmas bells
Christmas bells
All is well
All is well

Kathleen James

Undercover Guide

The Holy Spirit

That I know

Can travel in disguise

He uses the things of this world

You'll see him if you try

Like water taking any shape

Living water is his name

He will tell you the future

He will tell you your name

He will not add to this world

But uses the world ever day

Do you see the signs in the stars?

His handiwork you see

Did you need a friend?

Did they stop by?

A coincidence?

No Sirree

Did that verse jump off the page

And pierce your heart?

Yes, he talks to you

Teacher, counselor, loving friend

He is here for you

But when he, the Spirit of truth, comes, he will guide you into all the truth. He will not speak on his own; he will only speak what he hears, and he will tell you what is yet to come. (John 16:13)

Say I Do

To young and old
To one and all
Harken to my cry
What I'm about to tell you
Makes a difference in your life
Choose now
You must decide
Between life and death
With all that is within me
I beg you
Choose life the best
Now begins the story
Of the Greatest One of all
The Supreme Ruler of the Universe
And why he has come to call
Let's start at the beginning
He was the very first
He created the Heavens
He created the earth
There was a war in heaven
Angels did rebel
They were defeated
And he sent them to hell

Alleluia

29

He created you, my friend
He is the giver of life
Adam and Eve in the garden fell
Now enters sorrow and strife
Because of His love
This is a love story after all
He has made a way
For us to be restored
To walk again in his presence
Again, to call him Lord
Now enters Jesus
This is the Father's plan
He walked on the earth
The only perfect God man
He took your sins upon Him
And offers you a trade
Yes, this is Heaven-sent
This is Heaven-made
You do not have to earn it
Only receive and say, I do
He will rejoice
He is waiting for you
He is immortal
And immortal you will be
With or without Him
Tell me now
Where will you be?

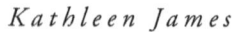

Kathleen James

30

Jesus

Jesus

Jesus

Come visit me

Jesus

Jesus

Come visit me

I want to walk beside you

I want to follow you

I want to do what you do

Tell me what I have to do

O o o o

My Lord

My Savior

My Friend

Keep me safe to the very end

And rescue me

E e e e

Jesus

Jesus

I wait for thee

Alleluia

City Lights

City lights

In the twilight

Truly look like jewels

Diamonds, rubies, sapphires

It is beautiful

Could this be

What he was describing

When he wrote so long ago

Of the city of Jerusalem

Laden with beautiful jewels

As he peers into the future

I peer into his past

As we peer together

At the city

Which is going to last

Having the glory of God: and her light was like unto a stone most precious, even like a jasper stone, clear as crystal. (Rev. 21:11)

Kathleen James

The Mark

The Lord looked on their forehead

And he saw their thoughts

The Lord looked on their hands

And he saw their acts

Fix these words of mine in your hearts and minds; tie them as symbols on your hands and bind them on your foreheads. (Deut. 11:18)

He also forced everyone, small and great, rich and poor, free and slave, to receive a mark on his right hand or on his forehead. (Rev. 13:16)

666

This calls for wisdom. If anyone has insight, let him calculate the number of the beast, for it is man's number. His number is 666. (Rev 13:18)

The number of the beast is man's number.

Man's number is

His sinful nature

Sinful thoughts

Sinful acts

His number is

Man man man

Or

Me me me

Selfishness

Just as the son of Man did not come to be served, but to serve, and give his life as a ransom for many (Matt. 20:28)

Kathleen James

Prophesy Unfolds

It is happening
It is happening now
Do you perceive it
Do you know how
It is unfolding
Under your nose
Every written promise
Every prophetic vow
Is happening
Is happening now
Connect the dots
And you will see
Clearer, better
Than even me
But we are safe
In his hands
Do not fear
Continue to stand
Cover your loved ones with prayer
Continue to love
Continue to care
Have courage my dear
We are almost there

———————

Alleluia

He Is Ours

He is great

He is awesome

And He is ours

Whatever you are struggling with

Leave it on the wayside

And focus on Him

Like Peter walking on the water

Walk over it

Focus on Him

He is great

He is awesome

And He is ours

Kathleen James

Star Wars

To all the *Star Wars* fans out there, do you remember the scene where Yoda raised the ship out of the swamp? Do you remember the scene when Obi Wan Kenobi blinded the guards thinking and told them they were not there? The same type of stories can be found in the Bible in 2 Kings 6 1-23:

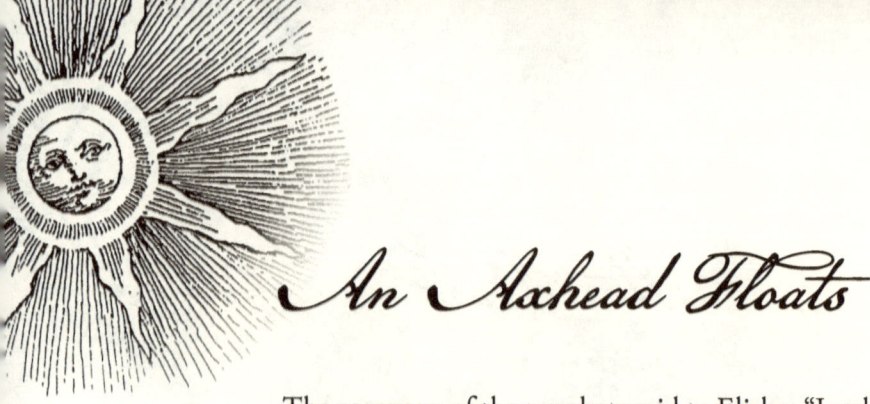

An Axhead Floats

The company of the prophets said to Elisha, "Look, the place where we meet with you is too small for us. Let us go to the Jordan, where each of us can get a pole; and let us build a place there for us to live."

And he said, "Go."

Then one of them said, "Won't you please come with your servants?"

"I will," Elisha replied. And he went with them.

They went to the Jordan and began to cut down trees. As one of them was cutting down a tree, the iron ax-head fell into the water. "Oh my lord," he cried out, "it was borrowed!"

The man of God asked, "Where did it fall?" When he showed him the place, Elisha cut a stick and threw it there, and made the iron float. "Lift it out," he said. Then the man reached out his hand and took it.

Kathleen James

Elisha Traps Blinded Arameans

Now the king of Aram was at war with Israel. After conferring with his officers, he said, "I will set up my camp in such and such a place."

The man of God sent word to the king of Israel: "Beware of passing that place, because the Arameans are going down there." So the king of Israel checked on the place indicated by the man of God. Time and time again Elisha warned the king, so that he was on his guard in such places.

This enraged the king of Aram. He summoned his officers and demanded of them, "Will you not tell me which of us is on the side of the king of Israel?"

"None of us, my lord the king," said one of his officers, "but Elisha, the prophet who is in Israel, tells the king of Israel the very words you speak in your bedroom."

"Go, find out where he is," the king ordered, "so I can send men and capture him."

The report came back: "He is in Dotham." Then he sent horses and chariots and a strong force there. They went by night and surrounded the city.

When the servant of the man of God got up and went out early the next morning, an army with horses and chariots had surrounded the city. "Oh, my lord, what shall we do?" the servant asked.

"Don't be afraid," the prophet answered. "Those who are with us are more than those who are with them."

And Elisha prayed, "O LORD, open his eyes so he may see." Then the LORD opened the servant's eyes, and he looked and saw the hills full of horses and chariots of fire all around Elisha.

As the enemy came down toward him, Elisha prayed to the LORD, "Strike these people with blindness." So he struck them with blindness, as Elisha had asked.

Elisha told them, "This is not the road and this is not the city. Follow me, and I will lead you to the man you are looking for." And he led them to Samaria.

After they entered the city Elisha said, "LORD open the eyes of these men so they can see." Then the LORD opened their eyes and they looked, and there they were inside Samaria.

When the king of Israel saw them, he asked Elisha, "Shall I kill them, my father? Shall I kill them?"

"Do not kill them," he answered. "Would you kill men you have captured with your own sword or bow? Set food and water before them so that they may eat and drink and then go back to their master." So he prepared a great feast for them, and after they had finished eating and drinking, he sent them away, and they returned to their master. So the bands from Aram stopped raiding Israel's territory.

Kathleen James

40

You Care

How beautiful you have become

How proud I am of you

Your heart is good

A decent soul

Hidden inside of you

You care

Yes, you care

This is not a fault

Your try to cover up this fact

By acting non-chalant

This world can be so cold and cruel

I'm sorry but it's true

Your strength has helped you persevere

Through some trying times

A heart that is hurt

Can be covered up

By callousness you see

But I know the treasure deep inside

No, you can't fool me

For there is one

———

Alleluia

Good and true

Decent is this soul

Who cares

Oh yes, who cares

To the benefit of us all

How beautiful you have become

How proud I am of you

Your heart is good

A decent soul

Hidden inside of you

You care, Oh you care

One who is good and true

I thank my God in heaven

Because he sent me you

Kathleen James

42

Worth It

I've really made a mess of things

Having my own way

I want to get it right

I want to start today

If Jesus Christ was standing in my shoes

If Jesus Christ was facing the decisions of my day

(I'm giving you a key my friend)

(I'm giving you a key my friend)

I want to do what Jesus did

I want to start today

If I can figure out what he would do

I'm gonna do that today

(The Holy Spirit will descend)

(The Holy Spirit will descend)

It's worth it in every way

Why did I wait so long

This gift

Why did I wait so long

And the rubber hits the road

Alleluia

The One

I know I don't have all the answers

I don't always do what's right

Sometimes I'm confused

Sometimes I try to justify

But I know The One who has the answers

I know The One who does what's right

I trust Jesus Christ my Savior

I know it's gonna be alright

My goal in life is to hear on judgement day the words, "Well done, my good and faithful servant."

Kathleen James

Prayers

Sunlight dawns at break of day

Bringing joy and triumph

As prayers of love and intrigue

Carry and inspire

Fire sparks within your heart

To the benefit of us all

Alleluia

Ever Present

Ever present, ever sound
The solid rock of love abounds
Failure taunts, regrets jeer
Reminding me of all the years
I look to you and have no fear
You wipe away every tear
Ever present, ever sound
Your voice is true, your love abounds
Failure and regret must leave
Chaos and disaster flee
Your power causes victory
Your voice is true, a solid rock
I look to you, my strength is locked
Ever present, ever sound
The love of God I have found
Your voice is true, your ways are right
Yes, you will win in every fight

You save me still

Love never fails…(1Cor13:8)

Kathleen James

Because of You

You forgave me

You saved me

By your power

By your might

I am renewed

My strength is locked

Because of you

I will win the fight

You save me still

Alleluia

A Mother's Prayer

A light in your eyes

A smile on your face

A song in your heart

And a spring in your step

Looks good on you, babe

Looks good on you

Oh my love

Looks good on you

I see you standing there

So fair

Watcha gonna do?

Oh my love

Watch gonna do?

Kathleen James

48

Let Them Play

To climb a tree

To skin a knee

To run around and whoop and holler

Till the day they get much taller

You have loved righteousness and hated wickedness, therefore God, your God, has set you above your companions by anointing you with the oil of joy. (Heb. 1:9)

Everyone who calls on the name of Jesus will be saved.

So just say, "Jesus."

Call out to him.

Alleluia

Choosing Christ

Two thoughts came to my mind when making the decision to choose Christ.

The first is, we are a family. And families belong together. In the vast expanse of the universe there is no telling what is out there. But this I am sure of, I want to be connected to my family. God created us, therefore we are the family of God. We belong together.

The second is, err on the side of reason. Let me explain. My brother and I had a conversation about life after death. He said if there is no life after death, you will cease to exist. It will not matter what you choose. But if there is life after death, it will matter a great deal what you choose. So be on the safe side and believe in life after death and choose Christ.

And after these things I heard a great voice of much people in heaven, saying, Alleluia; Salvation, and glory, and honor, and power, unto the Lord our God. (Rev. 19:1)

Kathleen James

What Time is It?

There is a time to zig

And a time to zag

The question is

What time is it?

Help me sir, to always follow the leading of your Holy Spirit, because you know what time it is.

Alleluia

A Time for Everything

3 for everything there is a season, and a time
  for every matter under heaven:

2 a time to be born, and a time to die;
  a time to plant, and a time to pluck up what
  is planted;

3 a time to kill, and a time to heal;
  a time to break down, and a time to build up;

4 a time to weep, and a time to laugh;
  a time to mourn, and a time to dance;

5 a time to cast away stones, and a time to
  gather stones together.
  a time to embrace and a time to refrain from
  embracing;

6 a time to seek, and a time to lose;
  a time to keep and a time to cast away;

7 a time to tear, and a time to sew;
  a time to keep silence, and a time to speak;

8 a time to love and a time to hate;
  A time for war, and a time for peace.

(Ecclesiastes 3 ESV)

Kathleen James

Only You Know

This day could go in so many different directions

Father, only you know

Where I should be

Where I should go

Take me there

As only you can

This is my prayer

This is my plan

Alleluia

Thermometer

Here is a thermometer for you

If you have peace and joy

You are walking close to God

If you have stress and strife

You are not walking close to God

Which means you need to have a talk with God

We have all been there

Just trying to help

Kathleen James

The Bible is Alive

You are an angel

A messenger from God

The wealth of knowledge you contain

Has yet to be told

You speak

You respond

I listen to your words

Someone else listens to the same words

But hears something different

You speak in parables

Every word written is also a parable

You are history

You are law

You are the owner's manual

You are a responding friend

If only we would listen

Filled with love

Filled with directions

A window to the future

A window to the past

Alleluia

A time machine

We can stand with him

Where He is

Your power has no limit

Every power in heaven and on Earth

Will bow

To your words

Your word never returns void

Your words have wings

Your words change things-always

Sometimes you speak instruction

I store away in my brain

Then when I need that instruction

You bring it to the forefront of my memory

It could be 20 years later

Sometimes you speak directly

Yes means yes

No means no

Sometimes you speak about my current situation

What I should do this very day

Sometimes you are tedious and boring

Hard for me to comprehend

Long lists of families

———————

Kathleen James

Laws, rules, and regulations

Something unseen happens

When you open the bible

Picture beams of light

Filled with power and miracles

Bursting forth

You are alive

The living word

The good news

You are the bible

Oh what a comfort you are

How reassured I am

How confident I am

As I stand on your word

The Comparison

Look at your Christmas tree.
See the lights
The tinsel
The beautiful decorations
Look at a plain evergreen tree
All green
All natural
Now here is the comparison
Think of yourself as the evergreen tree
All natural
When the Spirit of God comes to dwell
Within you
It's like the evergreen tree
Is turned into a Christmas tree
With the lights turned on
Do you see the Comparison?
Take it a step further
The evergreen tree had to die
To become the
Christmas tree
And now the Christmas tree
Has gifts of love for others
The presents under the tree

Kathleen James

Journey

Journey Lord Jesus

Make your way

To stand at the alter

The threshold

And look for me

Clothe me in

A robe of white

Take my hand and hold it

I Prayed for You

I prayed for you today.

I wanted you to know.

With tears and a humble heart,

I came before the throne.

I know my prayer was heard,

So expect to see a change.

Love and mercy flooding in.

Visiting angels today

The body of Christ will cross your path

And Satan falls like a stone.

Unlimited power and might

Here now bestowed.

Kathleen James

Nicene Creed

I believe in one God,

the Father almighty,

maker of heaven and earth,

of all things visible and invisible

I believe in one Lord Jesus Christ,

the only begotten Son of God,

born of the Father before all ages.

God from God, Light from Light,

true God from true God,

begotten, not made,

consubstantial with the Father;

through him all things were made

For us men and for our salvation

He came down from heaven,

and by the Holy Spirit

was incarnate of the Virgin Mary,

and became man.

For our sake

He was crucified under Pontius Pilate,

He suffered death and was buried,

Alleluia

61

and rose again on the third day

in accordance with the Scriptures.

He ascended into heaven and is seated

at the right hand of the Father.

He will come again in glory

to judge the living and the dead

and his kingdom will have no end.

I believe in the Holy Spirit, the Lord,

the giver of life, who proceeds from

the Father and the Son,

who with the Father and the Son

is adored and glorified,

who has spoken through the prophets.

I believe in one, holy, catholic

and apostolic Church.

I confess one baptism

for the forgiveness of sins

and I look forward to the resurrection

Of the dead

And the life of the world to come. Amen

Kathleen James